Praise for WHAT WAS HERE

"What I love most about this chapbook is how the poems in it are so keenly tied to the title, *What Was Here*. In it we step into moments where a firefly's light goes out, a branch whisks back into place after the departure of some unseen animal, or the remnants of a scarecrow's stake remain in the fields after the crops have been harvested. These moments, ensconced in Julie Warther's finely crafted contemporary haiku, remind us that life is happening all around us, and that we not only should, but need to stop and take notice before we, too, become something that once was here."

~ Ben Moeller-Gaa, author of *Wasp Shadows* (Folded Word) and *Blowing on a Hot Soup Spoon* (poor metaphor design)

"The twenty haiku in *What Was Here* are a celebration of autumn and winter, and Julie Warther's voice is present in all its power and richness. Lyrical and elegiac, Warther writes about the ordinary things of her native Ohio small-town, and the wilderness that survives both within her surroundings and within the reader."

~ Meik Blöttenberger

WHAT WAS HERE

Julie Warther

To Chase,
An amazing poet and a true friend!

settling
into a day lily...
the last of the light

Julie
Warther
4-24-15

FOLDED WORD

Meredith

Copyright ©2015 by Julie Warther and JS Graustein

All rights reserved. No part of this publication may be reproduced or distributed in any form or by any means, electronic or mechanical, without prior permission in writing from the publisher. Publisher hereby grants permission to reviewers to quote up to four lines from up to two poems in their reviews, and requests that hyperlinks to said reviews be e-mailed or physical copies mailed to the address below.

Requests for permission to make copies of any part of this work should be e-mailed to:
editors@foldedword.com, subject line "permissions"

ISBN-13: 978-1-61019-222-4

Folded Word
79 Tracy Way
Meredith, NH 03253
United States of America
WWW.FOLDEDWORD.COM

Cover and Design by JS Graustein
Author Photograph by Lois Mills
Titles set in Garamond Premier Pro
Text calligraphy in Carolingian hand

To Mom and Dad to fulfill a promise

WHAT WAS HERE

woodland trail
a notebook full
of blank pages

within the woods the wind

in the corral

a herd

of blackbirds

no longer able to move

our collie herds us

with her eyes

dad's directions

landmarks

that used to be

taking on water

the moon

fast approaching full

harvest eve...

raindrops dropping

through corn

autumn equinox...

a firefly

goes out

what was here

now gone – the branch

rights itself

whispers of winter

pass row by row

through the cornfield

last of the harvest
the scarecrow's stake
among the stubble

first day of winter ~
for the matinee performance
a sunset

frozen

in an icicle

a sky full of stars

sensing

before seeing...

overnight snow

bringing out the angel
in my child ~
fresh snowfall

dead of winter
deep in the forsythia

fluttering

midnight clear

a tiny spruce

swaddled in snow

many moons

on the snowcrust

lantern walk

midday

the sound of sunlight

dripping from icicles

Polaroid sky

waiting for what lies

beyond the mist

About the Author

JULIE WARTHER is an internationally recognized haiku and senryu poet currently serving as Midwest Regional Coordinator for the Haiku Society of America. Her poems have won numerous awards including the Robert Frost International Haiku Award (2012), The Polish International Haiku Competition (2013), and the Vancouver Cherry Blossom Haiku Invitational (2014). Her work is featured in many respected journals and anthologies including *A New Resonance 9: Emerging Voices in English-Language Haiku* (Red Moon Press 2015), *Haiku 2014* (Modern Haiku Press) and *The Red Moon Anthologies* (2013-2015). She lives a small-town life in Dover, Ohio where she fondly remembers what was here, enjoys what is, and hopes for what could be. To learn more, please visit her at:

TWITTER.COM/JULIEWARTHER

About the Calligrapher

JS GRAUSTEIN is the Editor in Chief of Folded Word, co-editor of the Twitter Lit anthology *On a Narrow Windowsill* (Folded Word 2010), and the author of *How to Write an Exceptional Thesis or Dissertation* (Atlantic Publishing Group 2012). She holds a Master of Science in Biology (Northern Illinois University, DeKalb), a Literary Publishing Certificate (Emerson College, Boston), and has studied translation under William O'Daly, noted translator of Pablo Neruda's late and posthumous work (Copper Canyon Press). Her calligraphy and photography have appeared on the covers of numerous hand-bound Signature Series chapbooks (Folded Word 2009-2013). This is her second chapbook rendered in the Carolingian hand. She lives amongst the trees in the picturesque highlands of Meredith, New Hampshire. To learn more, please visit her at:

GRAYESTONE.WORDPRESS.COM

Acknowledgements

Previous versions of the following poems were published in journals or recognized in contests. The author and publisher thank these organizations for their support.

Berry Blue Haiku: "in the corral"
Prune Juice: "no longer able to move"
Frogpond: "dad's directions"
A Hundred Gourds: "taking on water"
Mu: "what was here"
The Heron's Nest: "last of the harvest"
Runner-up, 2015 Golden Haiku Public Art Contest:
  "bringing out the angel"
2nd Place, 2012 Jane Reichhold International Haiku Contest:
  "midday"

The author would also like to thank JS Graustein and Folded Word, without whom this book would not have been possible. Heartfelt gratitude goes to Meik, Phyllis, Chase, Dan, Angie, Ellen, Pat, Ben, and Joe for their patience, guidance, honesty, and encouragement on this haiku journey.

The author and publisher would like to thank Rose Auslander, Casey Murphy, Barbara Flaherty, Liana Gott, Miran Reynolds, Megan Graustein, and Maryka Gillis for their assistance at the press during this chapbook's production.

More from the Folded Family

Wasp Shadows
by Ben Moeller-Gaa

Hints
by Rose Auslander

Catherine Sophia's Elbow
by Darla K. Crist

Sophronia L.
by Tim Bridwell

For a complete list of our titles plus multi-media presentations from this book, visit the Folded Word website: WWW.FOLDEDWORD.COM

To report typographical errors or problems with the functionality of this book, email:
EDITORS@FOLDEDWORD.COM

Want more information about our books, chapbooks, and zines? Want to connect with contributors from this book? No problem. Simply join us at a social media outlet near you:

weblog: FOLDED.WORDPRESS.COM
Facebook: WWW.FACEBOOK.COM/FOLDEDWORD
Twitter: TWITTER.COM/FOLDEDWORD
YouTube: WWW.YOUTUBE.COM/USER/FOLDEDWORD

We love to hear from our readers. Just send your thoughts via email to editors@foldedword.com with the subject line "WHAT WAS Feedback."

Cheers!